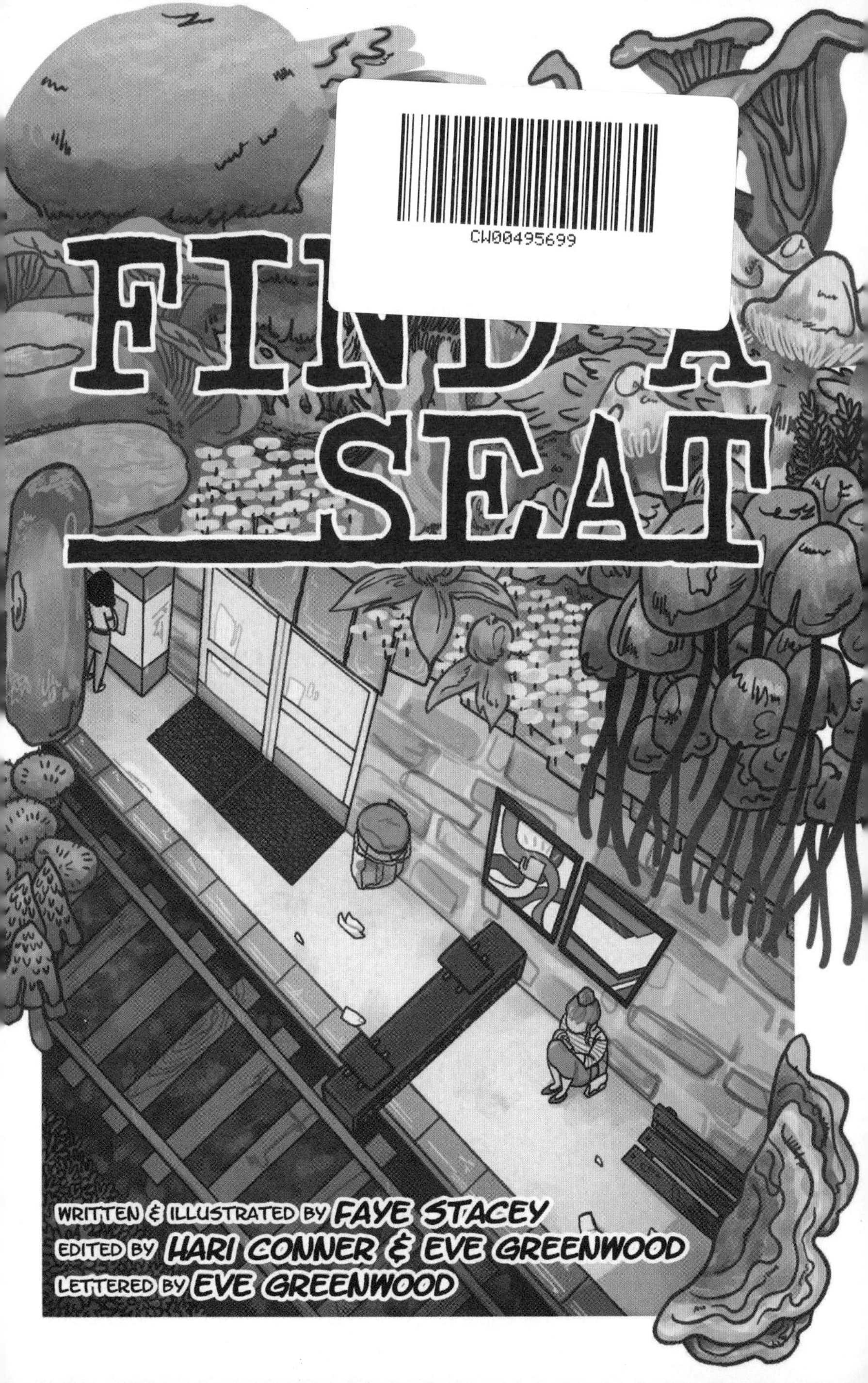
FIND A SEAT
WRITTEN & ILLUSTRATED BY FAYE STACEY
EDITED BY HARI CONNER & EVE GREENWOOD
LETTERED BY EVE GREENWOOD

SNIFF
SNIIIFFF
SPOOPY!

KKRRZZZT
IT'S YOUR TRAIN NEXT, OKAY?
BIG
ANDWICH

I'M SORRY SHE DUMPED YOU. IT SUCKS.
IT'S OKAY.
JUST DON'T KNOW HOW I'M GOING TO FACE HER AT UNI ON MONDAY.
DON'T THINK ABOUT UNI. DON'T THINK ABOUT MONDAY.
GET HOME AND SPEND THE WEEKEND SPOILING YOURSELF.
SHIT!
IF I DON'T HEAD NOW I'LL MISS MY BUS.
I'LL COME SEE YOU TOMORROW, OKAY?
THE NEXT TRAIN TO ARRIVE AT PLATFORM ONE...

...IS THE 10:42 TO GLENCORSE PARK.
CALLING AT...
PILRIG,
CHUG CHUG
FERNBANK, FOGNEUK,
BROOK,
AND GLENCORSE PARK.
K-CHUG CHUG
Glencorse Park 10:30
Brook, and Glencorse Park.
K-CHUG CHUG

AHEM.
TICKET, PLEASE.
OH!
UM...
YES, HERE.

UGH, WHY IS IT SO BUSY?
RAIL
I'M NOT STANDING THE WHOLE WAY.
K-SSSHHH

AHEM.
FIND A SEAT.

SPLORCH
AH!
OH, EURGH!
EWWW...
PLEASE LET THAT BE EMPTY.

OH GOD
OH GOD
OH GOD
THUNK
GA-THUNK
SQUISH

HEY!
HOW WOULD YOU LIKE IT IF I STOOD ON YOUR FACE WHY AREN'T YOU WATCHING WHERE YOU'RE GOING, I CAN'T BELIEVE HOW RUDE YOU ARE STANDING ON MY FACE LIKE THAT I'M RIGHT HERE--
YOU YOUNG PEOPLE ARE ALWAYS GLUED TO YOUR PHONES--
THEY DIDN'T EVEN EXIST WHEN I GOT HERE AND NOW--
EVERY OTHER WEEK IT'S SOME YOUNG PERSON STANDING ON MY FACE BECAUSE THEY'RE NOT WATCHING WHERE THEY'RE GOING--

LET'S SEE HOW WE GET ON IN HERE.
NOPE.
MAYBE.
DEFINITELY NOT.
MISS!
HEYYY.
pat pat
THERE'S PLENTY OF ROOM RIGHT HERE.

OH, NO THANK YOU.
WHYYYY
C'MON, I DON'T BITE.
NO, THANK YOU!
I JUST WANT TO TALK!
SQUEEZE
HEY!
CAN'T YOU SEE YOU'RE SCARING HER?

THANK YOU SO MUCH.
THERE'S A FREE SEAT DOWN THERE, HONEYBUNCH.
IF HE HASSLES YOU AGAIN, SEND HIM TO ME.
THANK YOU.
SO.

HOW DO YOU LIKE MY TRAIN?

W-WHAT?
HOW DO YOU LIKE MY TRAIN?
MY HAVEN FOR THE LOST AND WEARY?

THIS IS YOUR TRAIN?
YES.
WHERE IS IT GOING?
EVERYWHERE.
NOWHERE.
ANYWHERE IT'S NEEDED.
DIRECTIONLESS.
JOYLESS.
AND NOW THEY HAVE A PLACE WHERE THEY CAN JUST BE.
EVERYONE HERE IS LIKE YOU.
FREE FROM THE NEEDS OF OTHERS.
NEVER HAVING TO RETURN TO THEIR OLD, MISERABLE LIVES.

SAY IF...
YOU JUST COULDN'T FACE SEEING PEOPLE ANYMORE.
OR PERHAPS... A SPECIFIC PERSON?
EVERYONE HERE UNDERSTANDS THE DEPTHS OF YOUR PAIN.
AND THEY WILL SHARE THAT BURDEN WITH YOU.

AND IF I NEVER WANTED TO MAKE IT HOME...?
WE WOULD, OF COURSE, GIVE YOU SPACE HERE.
AND EVERYONE WOULD LEAVE ME ALONE?
BEEPA BEEP
IF THAT'S WHAT YOU WANT.
BEEPA BEEP
JUST THE CALM AND THE QUIET...
BEEPA BEEP

HM...
Stink brother
Aoife just messaged. She said she's put you on a train
Sorry
Puck is waiting for you to get back.
Text Message
UM, ACTUALLY...
IF IT'S OKAY...
I'D LIKE TO GO HOME.

SO...
LET ME BE SURE I UNDERSTAND CORRECTLY.
I DETOUR MY TRAIN...
TO COLLECT YOU AND PROTECT YOU IN YOUR LOWEST MOMENT.

I GIVE YOU A SPACE TO BE SAFE FOREVER...
FREE FROM THE SHACKLES OF YOUR MISERY-MAKERS.
AND YOU'RE REJECTING IT?
nod nod
VERY WELL.
HOWEVER, THERE IS ONLY ONE WAY TO ESCAPE MY DOMAIN.
glorb
TRIUMPH OVER MY GAME OF SKILL--
SHOOM
AND I'LL RELEASE YOU AT YOUR WILL.

BEAT THE FIRST FIVE LEVELS WITHOUT LOSING ALL THREE LIVES.
- IF YOU SUCCEED, I WILL TAKE YOU TO YOUR FRONT DOOR.
FAIL, HOWEVER...
Skull Swap
PLAY
AND YOU REMAIN WITH ME FOR ALL ETERNITY.

'SKULL SWAP'?
10,000 points
Lives
I USED TO HAVE DICE OF ANCIENT BONE--
BUT I GOT SICK OF CARVING NEW ONES EVERY TIME SOMEONE LOST ONE.
RICHARD'S VOCATION IN THE HUMAN WORLD WAS A CURIOUS PROFESSION: 'MOBILE DEVELOPER'.
SO HE HELPED ME CREATE A NEW CHALLENGE FOR THE MODERN ERA.
TO PLAY, YOU SIMPLY SWIPE THE GAME PIECES TO CREATE GROUPS OF THREE OR MORE!
BUT DON'T LET THE SIMPLICITY OF THE MECHANICS FOOL YOU.
IT IS FIENDISHLY DIFFICULT.

KEEP GOING, THEN.
50 bones
3 Lives
Collect 50 bones
50 bones
3 Lives

UGH!
3 Lives
2 Lives
YOU MANAGING?
I'LL GET IT NEXT TIME.
BLOOP!

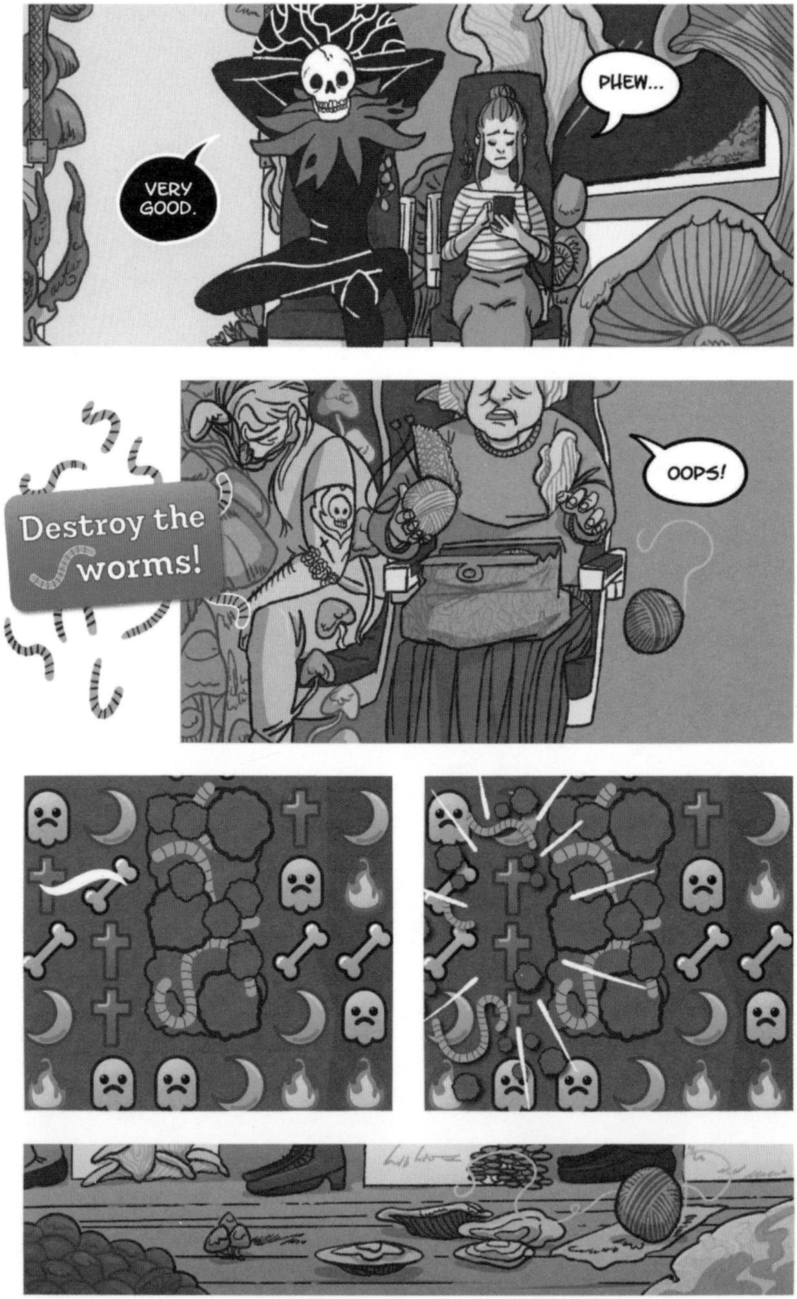
VERY GOOD.
PHEW...
Destroy the worms!
OOPS!

You Failed
TRY AGAIN
2 Lives
1 Lives
IF I LOSE THIS NEXT LIFE--
I'M STUCK HERE FOREVER.

12
worms
1
Lives
You Failed
TRY AGAIN
12
1
Lives
You Failed
TRY
swish
swish
17
worms
5
turns
remaining

ONLY FIVE TURNS LEFT...? THERE'S NO WAY I CAN DO THIS.
17 worms
1 Lives
5 turns remaining
ping!
NEED HELP?
5 MOVES
2 POWER-UPS
You're so close!
£5.99
WHAT?

NEED HELP?
5 MOVES
2 POWER-UPS
You're so close!
£5
worms
Lives
Ping!
PAYMENT SUCCESSFUL!
Thanks!

SUCCESS!
HEY!

206.039.270
points
1
Lives
SUCCESS!
LEVEL 5 COMPLETE
WHAT ARE YOU DOING?
WINNING.
WITH POWER-UPS?!
YOU DIDN'T SAY I COULDN'T!
HOW MANY HAVE YOU BOUGHT?
DIDN'T KEEP COUNT.
206.039.270
points
1
Lives
SUCCESS!
LEVEL 5 COMPLETE

OH, GOD... MY CREDIT CARD...
I'LL BE SPEAKING TO RICHARD ABOUT HOW TO GATE THAT OFF FOR FUTURE CONTESTANTS...
SIGH...
CONGRATULATIONS!
YOU HAVE BESTED MY CHALLENGE, AND HAVE WON YOUR FREEDOM, AS PROMISED.

I'D BETTER FIND THE CONDUCTOR.
WELL DONE.
I WILL REMEMBER THIS FOR A LONG TIME.

THIS IS YOU, I BELIEVE.
AND REMEMBER, EVEN A TINY REASON...
...IS STILL A REASON TO KEEP GOING.

THANK YOU.
MORGAN, IS THAT YOU?
KETTLE JUST FINISHED BOILING, SO POT OF TEA INCOMING!
WAS THE TRAIN BUSY?

Aoife Beefer
But like peasants invented salami!! Do other people not think about these things???
Haha!!! Noooo
Well I feel bad for the rest of you not able to wonder about the life you might be living parallell to like an old peasant in Tuscan Italy 200 years ago
Today
Got home safe xxx
Text Message
DORFELD!
OH, PUCK...
THANK YOU FOR BEING MY REASON TO COME BACK.

IT'S HARD, BUT...
I'LL TRY AGAIN TOMORROW.

# CONCEPT ART FROM 2021

## Death Insert

Violet Crowncup

Hollow ball underground
Bursts into crown above ground

Grow in coniferous & deciduous woodland
So garment should be mossy, pine needles & pine cones?

more open

fades into low opacity?

Almost the height of the train carriage

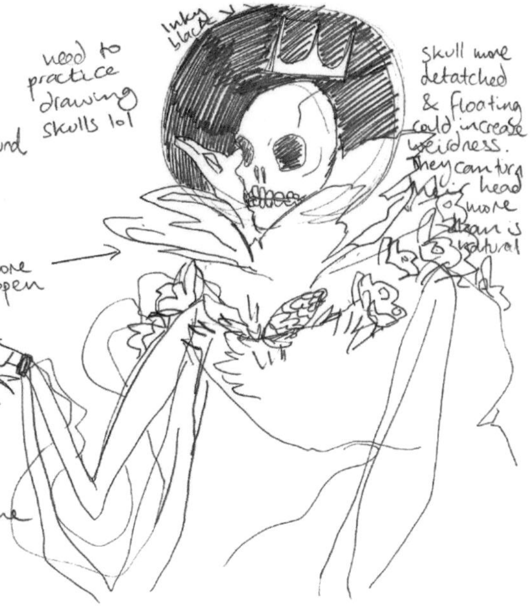

# ABOUT THE ARTIST

FAYE STACEY
IS A GLASGOW-BASED DESIGNER AND ILLUSTRATOR, WHO SPENDS THEIR TIME DRAWING CREATURES AND COMIC BOOKS. THEY'VE COLOURED BOOKS FOR MAD ROBOT COMICS, AND CREATED THEIR OWN WEBCOMIC *SUB TERRA*. WHEN NOT DRAWING THEY ARE USUALLY WRAPPED IN A BLANKET PLAYING VIDEO GAMES.

FAYESTACEY-ILLUSTRATION.CO.UK